W9-BEH-886

TIME
FOR KIDS
READERS

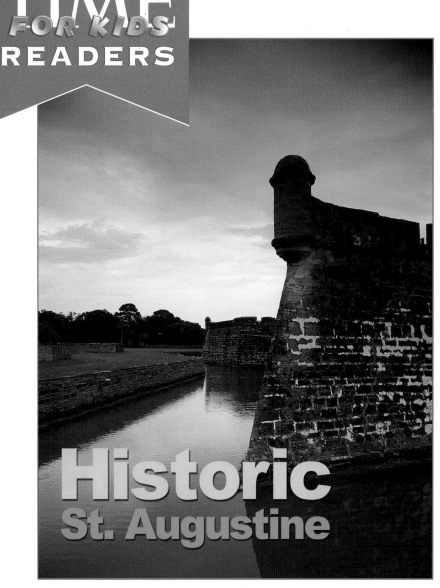

Historic
St. Augustine

by Jeri Cipriano

Orlando   Austin   Chicago   New York   Toronto   London   San Diego

Visit *The Learning Site!*
www.harcourtschool.com

This is St. Augustine, Florida. St. Augustine was settled by Spain. The city is the oldest in what is today the United States.

Mississippi

South
Carolina

Georgia

Alabama

ATLANTIC
OCEAN

St. Augustine

GULF of MEXICO

Florida

Don Juan Ponce de León, a
Spanish explorer, reached land
in North America in 1513. He
called it La Florida. Soon after,
the village of St. Augustine was
founded.

3

St. Augustine is like a living history museum. Here, in a special area called the Spanish Quarter village, people dress as Spanish settlers did hundreds of years ago.

Visitors come to hear about life in old St. Augustine. Children there helped their families. When their work was done, the children played games like marbles.

Families lived in small houses. Some only had two rooms. One room was used for sleeping and indoor activities. The other room was used for cooking. This house was built around 1790.

The oldest wooden schoolhouse in the United States is in St. Augustine. It was built in the 1700s. In 1788, it became the first school to bring girls and boys together to learn.

Each year, from November through January, St. Augustine becomes a city of lights. The people of St. Augustine are proud of their rich heritage.